Instantly compare any two places on Earth!

Activity Book

OverlapMaps takes a map of one part of the world and overlaps it on a different part of the world!

Instantly compare any two places on Earth!

Activity Sheets

Editorial
Sunflower Education
Design
Cynthia Hannon Design
ISBN-13: 978-1-937166-19-9
ISBN-13: 1937166198
Copyright © 2014
Sunflower Education. All rights reserved. Printed in the U.S.A.

Contents

A Note to Parents and Teachers

Using OverlapMaps.com

Understanding OverlapMaps.com	2
Why Make OverlapMaps?	4
How to Make OverlapMaps	5
Manipulating OverlapMaps	7
Saving and Sharing OverlapMaps	9

Lessons

Lesson 1: Map Projections	12
Lesson 2: Understanding Oceans	18
Lesson 3: Understanding Continents	22
Lesson 4: Understanding Nation-States	27
Lesson 5: Nation-States—Big and Little	29
Lesson 6: Understanding States and Provinces	32
Lesson 7: The United States—Big and Little States	34
Lesson 8: Canada—Big and Little Provinces	37
Lesson 9: Explore Your World	39
Lesson 10: More Fun Maps	40

Answer Key   43

A Note to Parents and Teachers

Thank you for considering using OverlapMaps.com to help the young people in your life get a better sense of the size and shape of their world.

About the Website: OverlapMaps.com

OverlapMaps.com enables the user to take a map of one part of the world and overlap it onto a different part of the world.

OverlapMaps.com has been used by thousands of homeschoolers and hundreds of schools. Interestingly, many of the website's visitors are adults who "have always wondered" how big a place was compared to more familiar terrain. So, hopefully, you will enjoy these activities as much as your kids.

Please be aware that there is advertising on the website. We control the website and the only ads are for our small educational publishing company, Sunflower Education. The carousel of books at the top links to specific books on Amazon, and the banner ads at the bottom, which change each time the page is refreshed, link to the following websites:

- our publishing company, SunflowerEducation.net
- our activity book series, WorldRecordsBooks.com
- our outdoor learning series, ActualSizeBooks.com
- our cookbook series, CookingUpHistory.com
- our company page at Amazon.com

As parents ourselves, we encourage you to preview these websites, but everything is G-rated.

About These Activity Sheets

These activity sheets are designed to be used in conjunction with the website OverlapMaps.com. They provide a *macro* sense of the world for students to provide an overall framework for their social studies learning. This teaching technique borrows from the work of Kieran Egan and from the idea of meaningful learning—which is a fancy way of saying "if you understand the big, you will understand the little," and "build on what kids know."

Essentially, a student working through these pages will learn, or have his or her knowledge reinforced, in this macro-to-micro order:

The World

Earth is a planet.
    Most of the planet is covered by the world ocean.
        The world ocean is divided among five oceans (details about each).
    Earth not covered by the world ocean is the land.
        The land is divided among seven continents (details about each).
            The continents are divided among about 200 nation-states.
            Nation-states are the basic building blocks of today's world.
            Nation-states have four defining characteristics.
            Nation-states vary in shape and size.
                Nation-states are divided into states and provinces.
                    States and provinces vary in shape and size.
                      My state or province is among these.
                          Here is where I stand in relation to my state or province, nation-state, continent, land, and planet.

A Child

Notice how the order promotes an overall, big-picture understanding. This is more crucial than ever in today's hyperconnected world. If the student hears that Russia is threatening Ukraine, for example (or any of the other countless news items that involve nation-states), the student will view that information through the lens of how and why humans have organized the land—and where he or she is in the scheme of things.

Notice, too, that the ideas extend from basic (definition of continents) to sophisticated (sovereignty of a nation-state). This is by design. Every child is different. Some older teens need reminders of basic information, and some of the little ones can handle surprisingly sophisticated information. Each student will reach a unique depth of understanding.

The last item on the list, and as important as the others, is this:

imagination and free time

We hope your kids (and you) spend some time just playing around on OverlapMaps.com!

How to Use These Activity Sheets

You have two basic options:

- Work through these sheets with your student or students;
- Have your student or students work independently.

We have seen grownups work closely with kids through the first section, "Using OverlapMaps.com," and then turn the kids loose for the rest. (The lessons are all speaking directly to the learner.) It is entirely up to you.

Know, too, that although the lessons are arranged in a logical hierarchy, you are the best judge of what the kids in your care need or want to learn. Feel free to jump around!

Using OverlapMaps.com

The following pages will guide you through understanding OverlapMaps.com.

You will learn what an OverlapMap is, why OverlapMaps are useful, and how to create, modify, save, and share your OverlapMaps.

Understanding OverlapMaps.com

OverlapMaps.com is a website. To keeps things simple, we will call OverlapMaps.com just "OverlapMaps" for short.

OverlapMaps only does one thing. But it does that one thing extremely well!

What OverlapMaps does is take a map of one part of the world and overlaps it on a different part of the world.

Overlap something means to "put it on top of." Some people say overlay instead. We like overlap, because it rhymes with map! And we call the maps you create OverlapMaps.

For example, you can take a map of France and overlap it onto a map of the United States. The map you create is an OverlapMap. On the map below, the purple shape is the correct size and shape of France if it were magically transported to the middle of the United States.

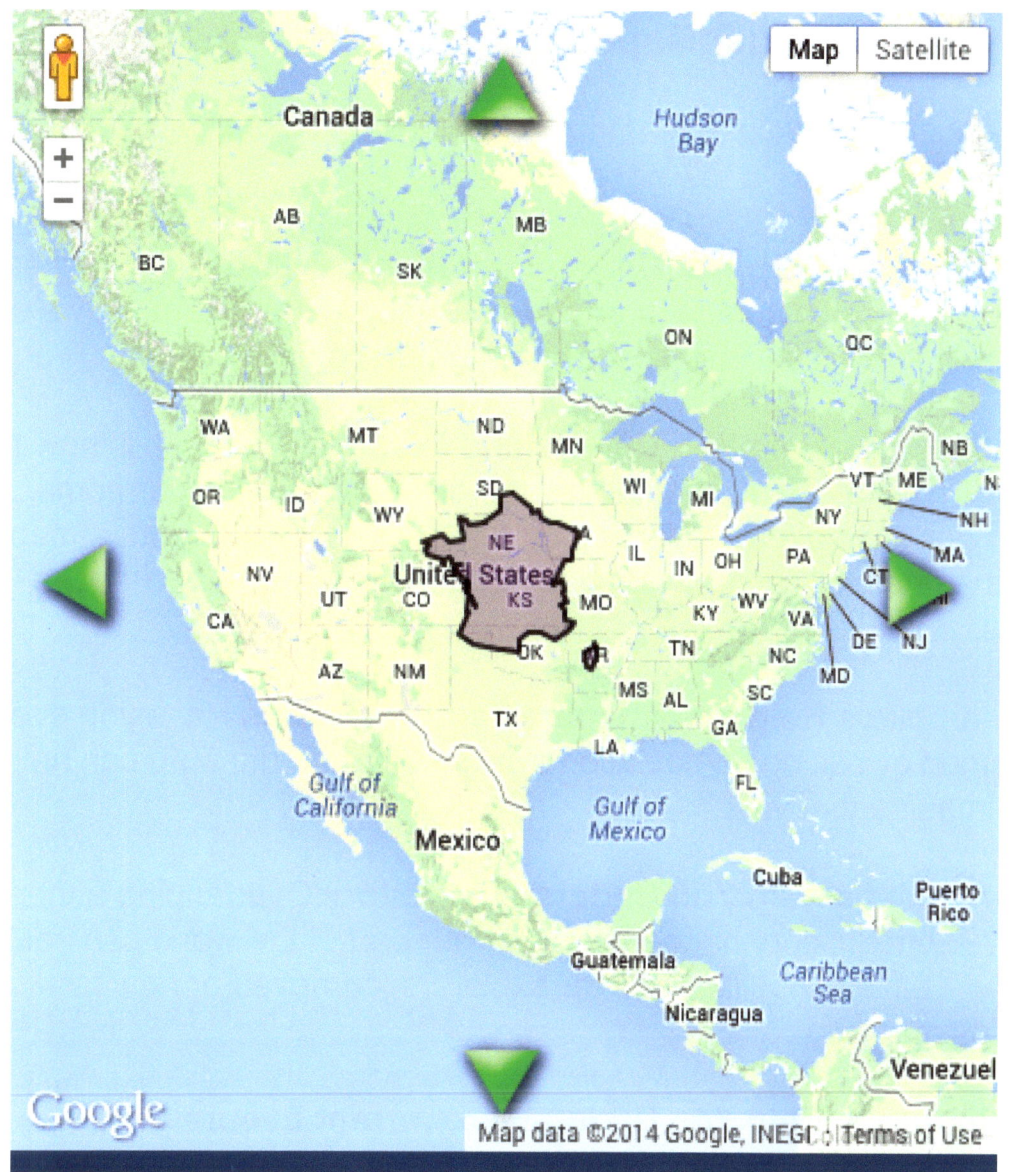

This shows a map of France overlapped onto United States

Why Make OverlapMaps?

Why would you want to create an OverlapMap? That's a good question. Here are a few good answers!

OverlapMaps Help You Understand Relative Size *Relative* means "in relation" or "in comparison" to each other. In our example, we can see that the United States is much larger in comparison than France.

OverlapMaps Help You Understand Distance Distance is how far apart things are. You might know the distance across your home state, for example. By overlapping a map of your state onto a map of another state or country, you can get a better sense of distances there.

OverlapMaps Help You Imagine Faraway Places Have you ever dreamed of visiting someplace far away? An OverlapMap can help you imagine that visit.

OverlapMaps Help You Understand History Overlapping a map where some history happened onto your part of the world can help you visualize things like how far explorers journeyed or how far armies marched.

OverlapMaps Help You Understand Current Events Viewing a map of another country where important events are taking place overlapped on your own country can help you better interpret those events.

OverlapMaps Help You Understand Your World!

How to Make OverlapMaps

Making OverlapMaps at **OverlapMaps.com** is as simple as 1-2-3!

1. Select the map you want on top from the left dropdown menu.
2. Select the map you want on bottom from the right dropdown menu.
3. Click the big green arrow.

Your map will appear in the map window to the right.

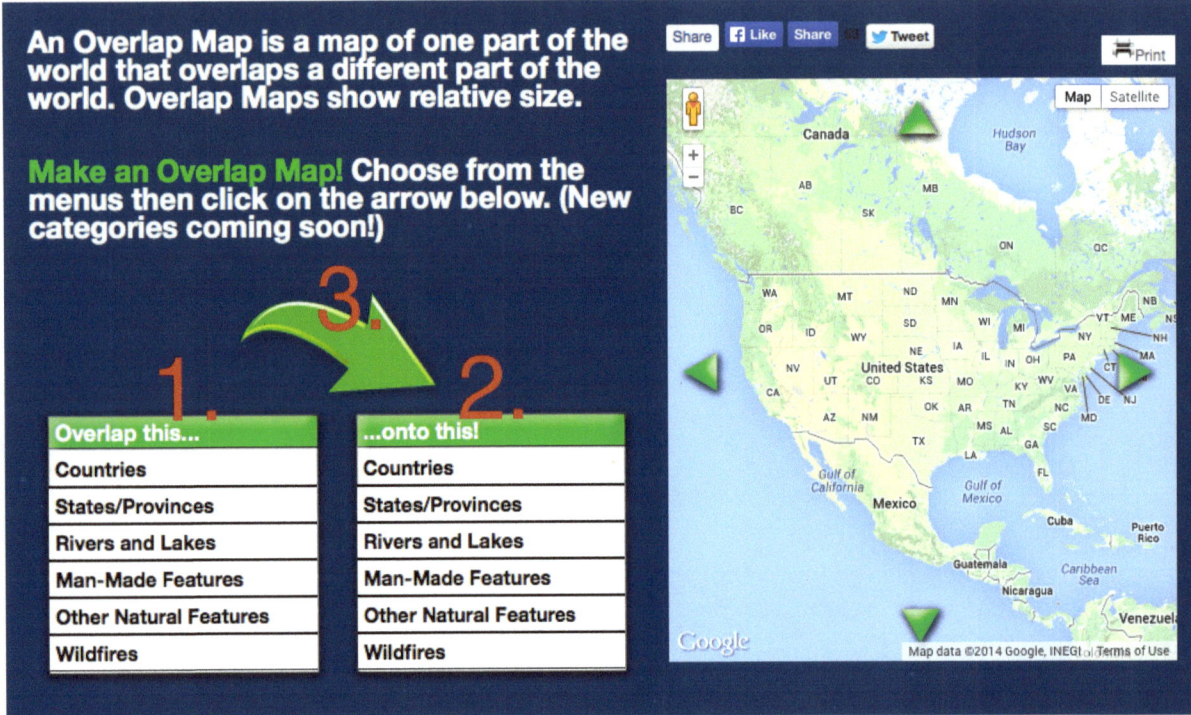

Manipulating OverlapMaps

After you have made your OverlapMap, you can manipulate it in several ways.

1. Move the Map You can move the overlapped map around the bottom map by using the green arrows at the top, bottom, left, and right of the map.

2. Zoom In and Out You can zoom in and out using the plus and minus buttons at the top left of the map.

3. Map and Satellite Views You can switch between Map and Satellite views by using the labeled buttons at the top right of the map.

4. Focus on One Place You can center the map on either of the two places you selected by clicking on the underlined names in the text below the map.

5. Streetview You can use Streetview by dragging the peg man from the upper left of the map onto any blue street.

Saving and Sharing OverlapMaps

There are several ways to save and share the OverlapMaps you create.

1. Save Save your OverlapMap by clicking on the grey Share button. This will generate a shortened URL that will permanently link to your OverlapMap. You share this link with as many people as you want.

2. Facebook You can share your OverlapMap on Facebook by clicking the blue Share button. You can also like OverlapMaps by clicking on the Like button.

3. Twitter You can Tweet your OverlapMap on Twitter by clicking on the Tweet button.

4. Print You can print your OverlapMap by clicking on the Print button.

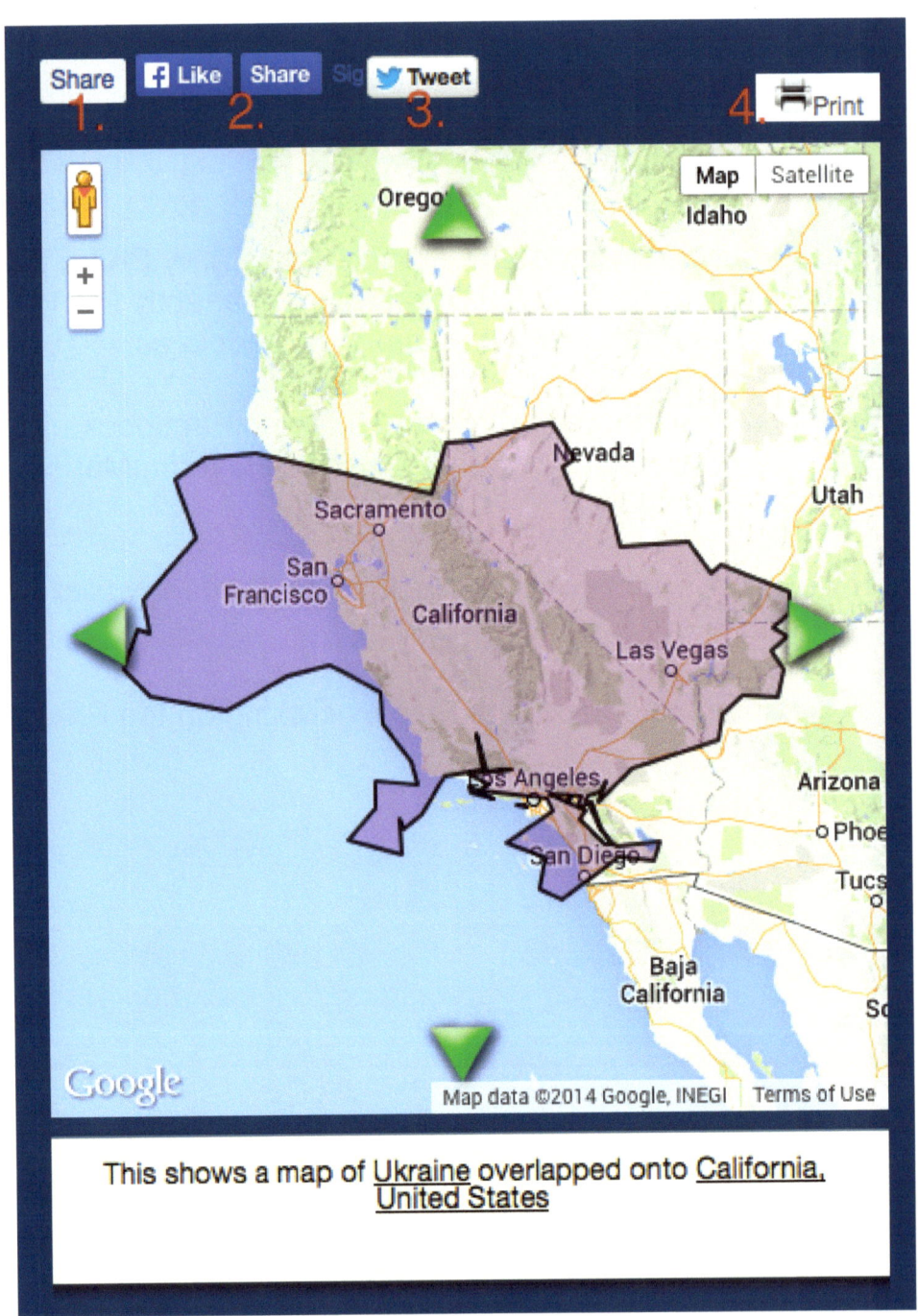

Lessons

The following pages will guide you as you use OverlapMaps.com to learn about map distortion, continents, oceans, nation-states, and other aspects of our world.

Lesson 1: Understanding Map Projections

DIRECTIONS: Read the article and study the maps. Then complete Quick Review 1.

All maps are flat representations of the Earth's curved surface. So all flat maps **distort,** or stretch, the curved surface of the Earth to make it flat. (Think about taking the curved peel off of an orange and making it lie flat on a countertop. You'd have to tear and stretch the peel to force it to lie down. That's what mapmakers, or **cartographers,** have to do.)

There are different ways of "flattening" the earth's surface to make a map. Each one is called a **projection** (because the curved surface is being projected onto a flat surface). The type of map projection that you see on OverlapMaps is called a **Mercator projection.**

Like all projections, the Mercator projection distorts something to make the curved surface lie down flat. The Mercator projection is very good at accurate distances and directions (It was made for European explorers sailing the seas). But what it does distort is size. See if you can find Greenland and South America below. Look at how much bigger than South America Greenland appears to be!

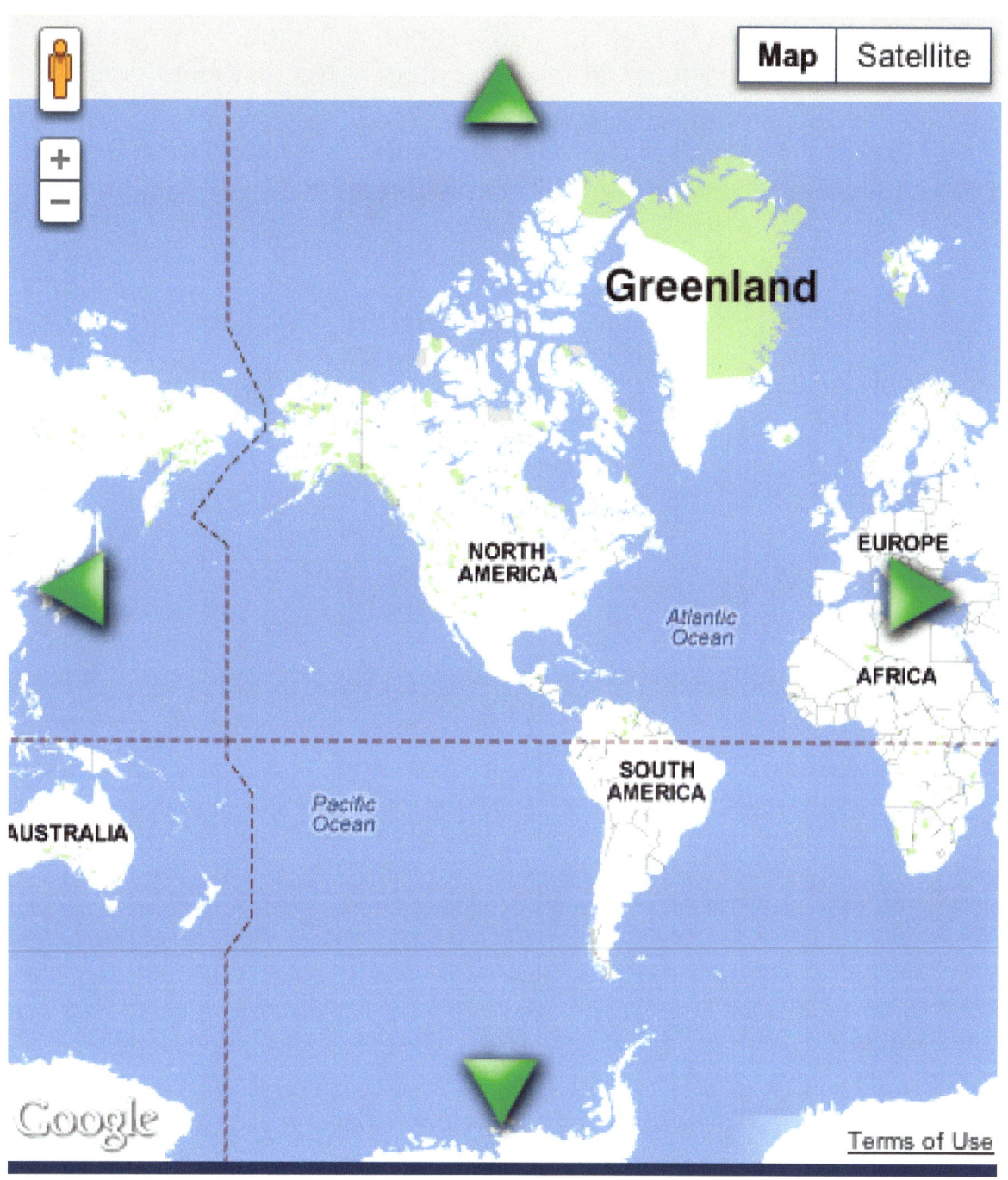

But, you know what? In reality, South America is bigger. Like EIGHT TIMES bigger! It just looks smaller because of the distortion.

You can see this distortion when you overlap Greenland onto Brazil in South America. (Look at the little purple Greenland.)

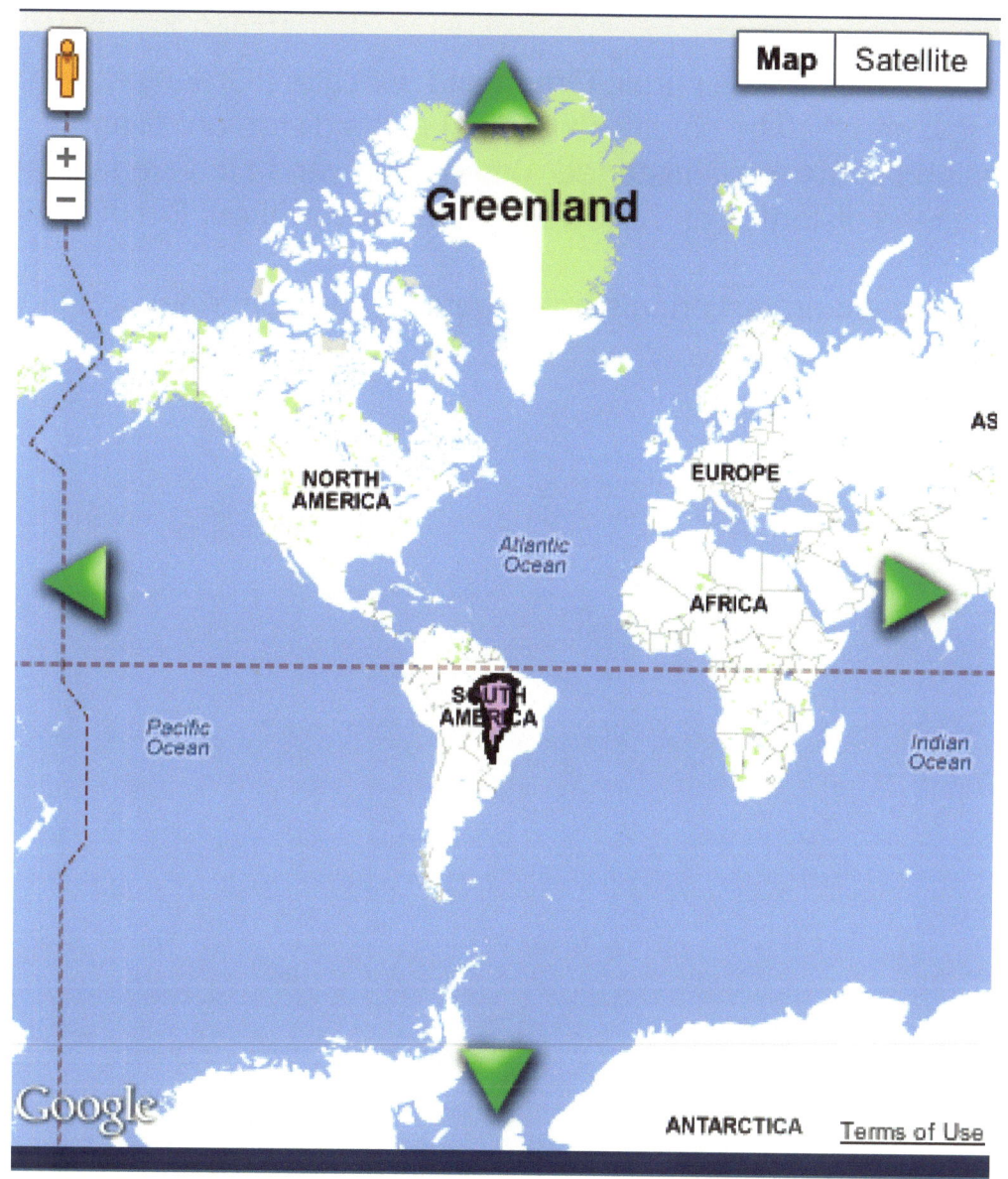

This shows a map of Greenland overlapped onto Brazil

That's how big Greenland really is, without the distortion.

But now compare little purple Greenland with giant Greenland at the top. How can they be so different? That is the distortion. Giant Greenland at the top is distorted. When you overlap it, OverlapMaps corrects the distortion and shows it actual size, without the distortion.

On a Mercator projection, distortion gets worse the farther you get from the Equator.

Quick Review 1

1. Why are all flat maps distorted?

2. What does a cartographer do?

3. What is a map projection?

4. What map projection does OverlapMaps use?

5. What does this projection distort?

Lesson 2: Understanding Oceans

DIRECTIONS: Go to OverlapMaps.com. Zoom the map out. Locate each of the oceans as you read about it. Then complete Quick Review 2.

As you know, the Earth is a planet, a giant ball of rock and other materials floating in space.

Most of the Earth is covered by water. This great body of water is called **the world ocean.** The world ocean is also called **the sea.** The continents divide the world ocean into five parts. Each part is an ocean with its own name.

Pacific Ocean
Atlantic Ocean
Indian Ocean
Southern Ocean
Arctic Ocean

Oceans Facts

How Big? Oceans cover more than two-thirds of the Earth.
How Deep? The oceans have an average depth of 13,000 feet. The deepest point in the ocean is 35,840 feet deep.
How Important? Oceans are needed for life on Earth. This is because the oceans help keep the air at a good temperature. They also provide moisture for rain.
Did You Know? People need the oceans. The oceans provide us with food. Ships carry people and goods between continents. People like to ride boats and swim in the oceans. Half of all the people in the world live close to an ocean.

The Five Oceans

1. The Pacific Ocean

How Big? The Pacific Ocean has an area of 66 million square miles. The Pacific is the largest ocean.
How Far? The Pacific Ocean's longest distances are 8,600 miles north to south and 15,000 miles east to west.
How Deep? The Pacific Ocean has an average depth of 13,000 feet. Its deepest spot is 35,840 feet deep.
Did You Know? Ferdinand Magellan was an explorer. He sailed the Pacific. He found calm water and gentle winds. "Pacific" means calm and gentle.

2. The Atlantic Ocean

How Big? The Atlantic Ocean has an area of 34 million square miles. The Atlantic is the second-largest ocean.
How Far? The Atlantic Ocean's longest distances are 13,000 miles north to south and 5,500 miles east to west.
How Deep? The Atlantic Ocean has an average depth of 12,000 feet. Its deepest spot is 28,232 feet deep.
Did You Know? The ancient Romans named the Atlantic. The Atlas Mountains were at the edge of their land. Atlantic means "beyond the Atlas Mountains."

3. The Indian Ocean

How Big? The Indian Ocean has an area of 27 million square miles. The Indian is the third-largest ocean.
How Far? The Indian Ocean's longest distances are 5,500 miles north to south and 6,200 miles east to west.
How Deep? The Indian Ocean has an average depth of 13,000 feet. Its deepest spot is 23,812 feet deep.
Did You Know? The Indian Ocean is named after India. India is a huge piece of land that sticks into the ocean from the continent of Asia.

4. The Southern Ocean

How Big? The Southern Ocean has an area of 9 million square miles. The Southern Ocean is the fourth-largest ocean.
How Deep? The Southern Ocean has an average depth of 15,000 feet. Its deepest spot is 23,737 feet deep.
Did You Know? You can not sail "across" the Southern Ocean. This is because the continent of Antarctica is in the middle of the Southern Ocean. The Southern Ocean surrounds Antarctica.

5. The Arctic Ocean

How Big? The Arctic Ocean has an area of 5 million square miles. The Arctic is the smallest ocean.
How Far? The Arctic Ocean's longest distance is 2,600 miles across.
How Deep? The Arctic Ocean has an average depth of 4,000 feet. Its deepest spot is 15,305 feet deep.
Did You Know? The Arctic Ocean is in a part of the world that is always cold. Much of the surface of the ocean is frozen into ice. You can walk on the ocean!

SOURCE: Oceans—A Bulletin Board in a Book!

Quick Review 2

1. What is the relationship among the world ocean and the five named oceans?

   _____
   _____
   _____

2. List the five oceans, from largest to smallest.

   1. _____
   2. _____
   3. _____
   4. _____
   5. _____

3. Which is the biggest and deepest ocean?

   _____

4. Which ocean is named for a mountain range?

   _____

5. Which ocean surrounds Antarctica?

   _____

Lesson 3: Understanding Continents

DIRECTIONS: Go to OverlapMaps.com. Zoom the map out. Locate each of the continents as you read about it. Then complete Quick Review 3.

The part of the Earth that is not covered by water is called **the land.** The land is separated by oceans into seven huge pieces. The huge pieces of land are called **continents.** Each continent has its own name.

Continents Facts

How Many? There are seven continents.
How Big? Continents cover about one-third of the Earth! The biggest continent is Asia. The smallest one is Australia.
How Important? Continents form the land of which almost all people live. Plants and animals also live on the land. Rivers and lakes that flow across the land give us water.
Did You Know? A lot of the land is not part of any continent. These are the many islands in the Pacific Ocean. There are almost 30,000 of them! These islands are called Oceania. They range in size from very small to very large.

The Seven Continents

1. Asia

How Big? Asia is about 17 million square miles. It is the biggest continent.
How Far? Asia's longest distances are 6,000 miles east to west and 5,400 miles north to south.
Who's There? About 4 billion people live in 50 countries in Asia.
Did You Know? More than half of all the people in the world live in Asia.

2. Africa

How Big? Africa is about 12 million square miles. Africa is the second biggest continent.
How Far? Africa's longest distances are 5,000 miles north to south and 4,700 miles east to west.
Who's There? About 1 billion people live in 53 countries in Africa.
Did You Know? Africa is home to many famous animals. Monkeys, gorillas, giraffes, hippos, zebras, lions, and tigers all live in Africa.

3. North America

How Big? North America is about 9.3 million square miles. North America is the third biggest continent.
How Far? North America's longest distances are 4,500 miles north to south and 4,000 miles east to west.
Who's There? About 530 million people live in 23 countries in North America.
Did You Know? The name "America" comes from an explorer. His name was Amerigo Vespucci. Over time, "Amerigo" became "America."

4. South America

How Big? South America is about 6.9 million square miles. South America is the fourth biggest continent.
How Far? South America's longest distances are 4,800 miles north to south and about 3,200 miles east to west.
Who's There? About 400 million people live in 12 countries in South America.
Did You Know? Most people in South America speak Spanish. That is because people from Spain took over most of the continent long ago.

5. Antarctica

How Big? Antarctica is about 4.7 million square miles. Antarctica is the fifth biggest continent.
How Far? Antarctica's longest distance is about 3,500 miles across the continent.
Who's There? Only a few people live in Antarctica. It is very cold there. At any time, about 3,000 scientists are in Antarctica doing research.
Did You Know? Antarctica is the coldest, driest, and windiest continent. That is why few people live there. At any time, about 3,000 scientists are in Antarctica doing research.

6. Europe

How Big? Europe is about 4 million square miles. Europe is the sixth biggest continent.
How Far? Europe's longest distances are about 4,000 miles east to west and about 3,000 miles north to south.
Who's There? About 700 million people live in 48 countries in Europe.
Did You Know? Europe is one of the smallest continents in size. But it is one of the biggest in population.

7. Australia

How Big? Australia is about 3 million square miles. Australia is the smallest continent.
How Far? Australia's longest distances are about 2,500 miles east to west and about 1,950 miles north to south.
Who's There? About 21 million people live in one country in Australia.
Did You Know? Australia is the only continent that has only one country. Both the country and the continent are called Australia.

SOURCE: Continents—A Bulletin Board in a Book!

Quick Review 3

1. List the seven continents, from largest to smallest.

1. _____
2. _____
3. _____
4. _____
5. _____
6. _____
7. _____

2. The word continent comes from the ancient Latin phrase *terra continens,* which means "continuous land." Why is this appropriate?
_____

3. Which continent is also a country?
_____

4. Which continent do you live on?
_____

5. Which continent would you like to visit the most? Why?
_____
_____
_____
_____

Lesson 4: Understanding Nation-States

DIRECTIONS: Read to learn what a *nation-state* is. Then go to OverlapMaps.com. Zoom the map out to see that almost all of the land on Earth has been divided into nation-states. Notice that the lines that separate nation-states are called borders. Then complete Quick Review 4.

You have probably heard the word *country*. How many countries can you name? There are the United States, Mexico, and Canada in North America. There are Spain and Sweden in Europe. There are Egypt and South Africa in Africa. There are India and China in Asia. But that's just a handful. All told, there are about 200 countries in the world today. Sometimes, people use the word *nations* instead of countries.

A more accurate term than country or nation, however, is **nation-state**. Nation-states have four main characteristics:

1. Territory Territory is a defined area of land with borders.
2. Sovereignty Sovereignty means self-rule; nation-states rule themselves.
3. Government Nation-states have organized governments.
4. Population The population, or people, of a nation-state, share some culture or language.

There are about 200 nation-states in the world today. Each one has a government. Therefore, there are about 200 national governments in the world. Each of these national governments is very powerful. Most have armies. Many have police forces. They can have a great deal of control of what happens to the people in their territory.

Quick Review 4

1. List the four characteristics of a nation-state.

   1. _____

   2. _____

   3. _____

   4. _____

2. What are two common synonyms for nation-state?
   _____
   _____

3. Do you think the Earth's land has always been divided into nation-states? Explain your answer.
   _____
   _____
   _____
   _____

4. Which nation-state do you live in?
   _____

5. Which nation-state would you like to visit the most? Why?
   _____
   _____
   _____
   _____

Lesson 5: Nation-States—Big and Little

DIRECTIONS: Go to OverlapMaps.com and make OverlapMaps using various combinations of the nation-states (under "Countries" on the website) listed above. Also compare them to your home nation-state. Then complete Quick Review 5.

There are about 200 nation-states in the world.

The ten biggest nation-states (biggest first) are:

1. Russia
2. Canada
3. China
4. United States
5. Brazil
6. Australia
7. India
8. Argentina
9. Kazakhstan
10. Algeria

The ten smallest nation-states (smallest first) are:

1. Vatican City
2. Monaco
3. Nauru
4. Tuvalu
5. San Marino
6. Liechtenstein
7. Marshall Islands
8. Saint Kitts and Nevis
9. Maldives
10. Malta

The five nation-states closest to the middle in size are:

1. Czech Republic
2. Serbia
3. Panama
4. Sierra Leon
5. Ireland

Quick Review 5

1. Tell something you learned about nation-states by making OverlapMaps of them.

_____
_____
_____
_____
_____

2. Why might the nation-states vary so much in size?

_____
_____
_____
_____
_____

3. How does your country compare to the large, small, and medium ones of the world?

_____
_____
_____
_____
_____
_____
_____

Lesson 6: Understanding States and Provinces

DIRECTIONS: Read to learn about states and provinces. Then go to OverlapMaps.com. Identify several countries with states and provinces. Spend some time making a variety of OverlapMaps using states and provinces. Make OverlapMaps of states and provinces within the same nation-state and of states and provinces from different nation-states. Take note of any patterns you see or conclusions you can draw. Then complete Quick Review 6.

You might already know that the United States is made up of 50 states. **States** are found in nation-states that have a federal system of government. Under a federal system of government, the power of government is shared between a federal, or national government, and many state governments. Like the larger nation-states they are part of, states have clearly defined territories and borders and their own government. They are not, however, completely independent.

Like states, **provinces** are smaller divisions of nation-states. Sometimes, provinces have more power compared to states; other times they do not. It depends on the country.

Quick Review 6

Tell what you learned about states and provinces by making OverlapMaps of them. Do they have similar shapes and sizes, or are they very diverse? What do you think accounts for their shapes?

_____
_____
_____
_____
_____
_____
_____
_____
_____
_____
_____
_____
_____

Lesson 7: The United States—Big and Little States

DIRECTIONS: Go to OverlapMaps.com and make OverlapMaps using various combinations of the states listed. Also compare them to your home state or province. Then complete Quick Review 7.

There are 50 states in the United States.

The three biggest states (biggest first) are:

1. Alaska
2. Texas
3. California

The three smallest states (smallest first) are:

1. Rhode Island
2. Delaware
3. Connecticut

The two states closest to the middle in size are:

1. Iowa
2. New York

Quick Review 7

1. Tell something you learned about states by making OverlapMaps of them.

_____
_____
_____
_____
_____

2. Why might the states vary so much in size?

_____
_____
_____
_____
_____

3. How does your home state or province compare to the large, small, and medium American states?

_____
_____
_____
_____
_____
_____
_____

Lesson 8: Canada—Big and Little Provinces

DIRECTIONS: Go to OverlapMaps.com and make OverlapMaps using various combinations of the provinces listed above. Also compare them to your home state or province. Then complete Quick Review 8.

There are 13 provinces in Canada. Here they are, from biggest to smallest:

1. Nunavut
2. Quebec
3. Northwest Territories
4. Ontario
5. British Columbia
6. Alberta
7. Saskatchewan
8. Manitoba
9. Yukon
10. Newfoundland and Labrador
11. New Brunswick
12. Nova Scotia
13. Prince Edward Island

Quick Review 8

1. Tell something you learned about provinces by making OverlapMaps of them.

_____
_____
_____
_____
_____

2. Why might the provinces vary so much in size?

_____
_____
_____
_____
_____

3. How does your home state or province compare to the large, small, and medium Canadian provinces?

_____
_____
_____
_____
_____
_____
_____

Lesson 9: Explore Your World

Now that you're familiar with OverlapMaps, feel free to explore the website on your own.

DIRECTIONS: Go to OverlapMaps.com and make various OverlapMaps. As you do so, think about these questions:

What are you comparing?
Why are you comparing them?
Is anything surprising to you?

Then complete Quick Review 9.

Quick Review 9

Write down three interesting things you learned.

1. _____

2. _____

3. _____

Lesson 10: More Fun Maps

Do you enjoy maps? Do you think world records are cool?

DIRECTIONS: Go to:
   http://worldrecordsbooks.com/Interactive_Maps.html.
There are five maps to choose from. Simply click on the title to visit each map. Then complete Quick Review 10.

Amazing World Records of GEOGRAPHY

World's highest sand dunes, largest iceberg, most remote island, deadliest battle—and 17 more.

Amazing World Records of WEATHER

World's worst weather disaster, hottest place, greatest wind speed—and 17 more. PLUS, you can overlap a map of current weather conditions!

More maps on the next page!

Amazing World Records of HISTORY

World's oldest boat, earliest machine, deadliest battle—and 17 more!

Amazing World Records of LANGUAGE AND LITERATURE

World's first writing, language with the fewest words, oldest book, and 17 more!

Amazing World Records of SCIENCE AND TECHNOLOGY

World's oldest fossil, largest ship, longest bridge—and 17 more.

See the Quick Review on the next page!

Quick Review 10

Write down three interesting things you learned.

1. _____
_____
_____
_____
_____

2. _____
_____
_____
_____
_____

3. _____
_____
_____
_____
_____

Answer Key

Quick Review 1

1. Flat maps are distorted because they stretch the curved surface of the Earth to make it flat.
2. A cartographer make maps.
3. They way a cartographer chooses to project the curved surface of the Earth onto a map.
4. OverlapMaps uses a Mercator projection.
5. The Mercator projection distorts shape.

Quick Review 2

1. The world ocean is composed of the five named oceans.
2. The five oceans from biggest to smallest are:
    1. Pacific Ocean
    2. Atlantic Ocean
    3. Indian Ocean
    4. Southern Ocean
    5. Arctic Ocean
3. The biggest and deepest ocean is the Pacific Ocean.
4. The Atlantic Ocean is named for the Atlas mountain range.
5. The Southern Ocean surrounds Antarctica.

Quick Review 3

1. The seven continents from biggest to smallest are:
    1. Asia
    2. Africa
    3. North America
    4. South America
    5. Antarctica
    6. Europe
    7. Australia
2. Continents are huge pieces of land that can be thought of as continuous within themselves but separate from the other

continents.
3. Australia is the continent which is also a country.
4. Confirm correct answer.
5. Reward a thoughtful response.

Quick Review 4

1. The four characteristics of a nation-state are:
    1. territory
    2. sovereignty
    3. government
    4. population
2. Two common synonyms for nation-state are country and nation.
3. Reward a thoughtful response. The modern nation-state is a relatively new development, historically. Nation-states as we know them today began to emerge in the 15th century. Consider having students research and report on the historical development of the nation-state.
4. Confirm correct answer.
5. Reward a thoughtful response.

Quick Review 5

1. Reward a thoughtful response.
2. Reward a thoughtful response. Nation-states are the result of hundreds of years of historical development influenced by culture, conflict, and geography.
3. Confirm correct answer.

Quick Review 6

Reward a thoughtful response. The shape of states and provinces are diverse and are the result of hundreds of years of historical development affected by culture, conflict, geography, and governing. Challenge students to research and report on the reasons for the size and shape of their home state or province.

Quick Review 7

1. Reward a thoughtful response.
2. Reward a thoughtful response. The shape of the states are the result of historical development affected by culture, conflict, geography, and governing. Challenge students to research and report on the reasons for the size and shape of their home state, or a state of their choice.
3. Confirm correct response.

Quick Review 8

1. Reward a thoughtful response.
2. Reward a thoughtful response. The shape of the states are the result of historical development affected by culture, conflict, geography, and governing. Challenge students to research and report on the reasons for the size and shape of their home province, or a province of their choice.
3. Confirm correct response.

Quick Review 9

Reward thoughtful responses.

Quick Review 10

Reward thoughtful responses.

www.ingramcontent.com/pod-product-compliance
Lightning Source LLC
Chambersburg PA
CBHW042123040426
42450CB00002B/46